CONFORMED
TO CHRIST

A Catholic Discipleship
Small Group Discussion Guide

The Evangelical Catholic
Follow Jesus Series

www.evangelicalcatholic.org

Table of Contents

ST. PAUL AND HIS WORLD

"For us Paul is not a figure of the past whom we remember with veneration. He is our teacher, an Apostle and herald of Jesus Christ for us too."

-Pope Benedict XVI

This *Follow Jesus* study is dedicated to the study of the great St Paul. His mark on the Church is well documented through countless artistic pieces, multitudes of Christian Churches named in his honor, and reams of books and articles that wrestle with his thought. The artistry of St. Peter's Basilica, in the center of Vatican City, also reveals his mark. Lining the roof of the basilica are statues of the first apostles, as if looking down upon St. Peter's square. Two prominent apostles are not among these statues on the roof, however. St. Peter's statue is set apart and stands to the left of the main entrance to the basilica. His statue is much more dominant in stature than those on the roof. Strikingly, St. Paul's statue matches St. Peter's prominence on the other side of the entrance, a powerful statement of St. Paul's authority and centrality in Christianity. St. Peter was the leader of the early Church and the Apostle to the Jews. St. Paul was chosen by the Lord to be the Apostle to the Gentiles, to the known world beyond the Jewish community. Together, Sts. Peter and Paul represent the universality of the Church's mission to the world. The statue of St. Peter holds the keys of the Kingdom of God that Jesus figuratively gave him in the Gospel according to St. Matthew. St. Paul holds a sword. The sword sculpted into Paul's hand traditionally represents both Paul's eventual beheading and also the "Sword of the Spirit, the Word of God," which he wielded as a missionary and continues to wield as our teacher, apostle, and herald.

With a full one-third of the New Testament books in Holy Scripture claiming his authorship, he is our great teacher. As one commissioned by Jesus himself to establish the early Church, he is our apostle. By his words, which continue to pierce the world with the light of the Gospel, he is our herald. So great is the influence of St. Paul upon the Church that we have four feast days dedicated to honor his life during the liturgical year: one for his Conversion (January 25), one for his Shipwreck (February 10), one dedicated for both Sts. Peter and Paul (June 29), and one for the dedication of the Basilicas of St. Peter and St. Paul Outside the Walls (November 18).

Saint Paul and his World

In this six weeks of *Conformed to Christ*, we enter an unfamiliar and fascinating world. A clairvoyant slave girl follows St. Paul around town yelling about him. An excited crowd mistakes St. Paul and his missionary partner Silas for Greek gods. A miraculous earthquake frees Paul and Barnabas from imprisonment. There is even a shipwreck.

All this and many other tales are told in the book of Acts. Full of stories of Paul's travels to Ephesus, Philippi, Galatia, Rome and other places, this book tells of the people and places St. Paul evangelized, and to whom he wrote his famous letters. These letters were collected by the church and became the Pauline epistles of the New Testament, from which we will also read. (Epistle is from the Latin word for letter.)

All of these stories and letters reveal Paul's intense love for Christ and for the people to whom he brought the good news of Christianity. In the midst of temptation, trial, and torture he proclaims the love of God in Christ. Even while in the Philippian prison Paul revealed his steadfast commitment to Christ when he wrote, "For to me to live is Christ, to die is gain." If he lived, he looked forward to laboring for Christ with his Christian brothers and sisters. If he died, his faith assured him the gain of eternal life with Christ. Paul's zeal and faith, even in the face of cultural pressures, inspired the earliest Christians and continues to speak to Christians in our age. It will be helpful for your discussions, however, to understand some of the cultural dynamics of Paul's time in order to draw deeper meaning from his life.

Three different cultures influenced the early church described in Acts: Jewish, Greek, and Roman. A little information about these will help us understand what we are reading. St. Paul, Jewish himself, became the apostle to the gentiles. Gentiles were everyone who was not Jewish. Because Alexander the Great conquered most of the known world in the fourth century before Christ, many people spoke Greek and practiced Greek religions.

In the cities, temples dedicated to various Greek gods were the centers of worship. The god considered a protector of a city would have a large temple and following. This was the case in Ephesus with Artemis, goddess of the hunt. In Acts 19 we read of silversmiths anger because Paul and his missionary team drew people away from the worship of Artemis. This depleted their customer base for silver idols. The silversmiths started a riot by accusing St. Paul of proclaiming a foreign god, Jesus Christ.

In week four of *Conformed to Christ*, when the people of Lystra mistake St. Paul and Barnabas for the Greek gods Hermes and Zeus, it sounds strange to us now. Yet it is understandable that they would try to classify St. Paul's miraculous powers within familiar religious categories. The clash and confusion between the monotheism of Judaism and the polytheism of Hellenistic culture appears repeatedly throughout Acts.

Though St. Paul was Jewish, as of course were Jesus, all his apostles and probably most of his earliest disciples, we read in Acts of the Jews persecuting Paul after his conversion to Christianity. They often accuse him of false teaching and get him in trouble with the law. Though it seems that Jews and Jewish Christians co-existed in the synagogues in the early days of Christianity, eventually Christians were considered a heretical branch of the faith. Especially after the destruction of the second temple by the Romans in 70 A.D., Judaism struggled to maintain its identity. Divergent strains of thought such as Christianity were a danger to the very survival of their faith.

The law of the day was under the Roman emperor. In Acts we meet many Roman officials and soldiers, usually because Paul has been arrested yet again. As a Roman citizen, St. Paul had certain rights and privileges, including the right to take his legal case before the emperor. The end of Acts tells of Paul's travels to Rome to undergo trial there. Tradition holds that he died there.

Was Paul only Talking to Men?

Conformed to Christ uses the Revised Standard Version of the Bible (RSV) because it is endorsed by the Magisterium of the Catholic Church as a valid translation and is no longer under copyright, as is the New American Bible Revised Edition (NABRE) from which we read in church. Because the RSV is older, it contains some older translation traditions. For example, it uses the term "brothers" where newer translations might use "brothers and sisters."

New Testament Greek, like Spanish and other romance languages, uses the masculine form for any group that contains men. For example, there could be six sisters and one brother, and the Spanish would still be "los hermanos." Similarly, the Koine Greek would be "adelphos." There is no equivalent to this in English. We never denote a group of brothers and sisters by the word brothers. We might use the word "siblings" to refer to brothers and sisters, but we would not use it as a form of address. "Greetings, siblings!" sounds silly.

Except in circumstances where there may well have only been men, such as on board the ship during the storm, we can safely assume Paul speaks both to men and women, even if your Bible's translation says "brothers." He must have preached to them and evangelized them, because Acts tells of women converts to the faith, such as Lydia, the purple dyer, and Priscilla (or Prisca) who runs a house Church with her husband Aquila.

Many people experiment with changing "brothers" to "brothers and sisters" when they read these passages. Members of your group may feel so inclined.

Pope Benedict XVI: St. Paul Continues to Speak

The following excerpt is taken from Pope Benedict's June 28, 2008 homily to open the Catholic Church's Jubilee Year to St. Paul.

"For us Paul is not a figure of the past whom we remember with veneration. He is also our teacher, an apostle and herald of Jesus Christ for us too.

"Thus we are not gathered to reflect on past history, irrevocably behind us. Paul wants to speak to us – today…Let us not ask ourselves only: who was Paul? Let us ask ourselves above all: who is Paul? What does he say to me?

"In the Letter to the Galations, St. Paul gives a very personal profession of faith in which he opens his heart to readers of all times and reveals what was the most intimate drive of his life. "I live by faith in the Son of God who loved me and gave himself for me" (Gal 2:20). All Paul's actions begin from this centre. His faith is the experience of being loved by Jesus Christ in a very personal way. It is awareness of the fact that Christ did not face death for something anonymous but rather for love of him – of Paul – and that, as the Risen One, he still loves him; in other words, Christ gave himself for him. Paul's faith is being struck by the love of Jesus Christ, a love that overwhelms him to his depths and transforms him. His faith is not a theory, an opinion about God and the world. His faith is the impact of God's love in his heart. Thus, this same faith was love for Jesus Christ."

As we enter into this six-week series together, let us open ourselves to be impacted along with Paul by the love of God in Jesus Christ. Jesus lived, died, and rose from the dead so that we could know and experience this great love. Like Paul, we look to Jesus in order to be transformed by this truth—God knows our name and gave his Son for each of us so that we could live abundant, fulfilled lives in Him.

LOVE

WEEK 1

"For I am sure that neither death, nor life, nor angels, nor principalities, nor things present, nor things to come, nor powers, nor height, nor depth, nor anything else in all creation, will be able to separate us from the love of God in Christ Jesus our Lord."

–Romans 8:38

Opening Prayer

Have someone read the following passage of Scripture aloud for our opening prayer.

1 Thessalonians 3:9-13

[9] For what thanksgiving can we render to God for you, for all the joy which we feel for your sake before our God, [10] praying earnestly night and day that we may see you face to face and supply what is lacking in your faith? [11] Now may our God and Father himself, and our Lord Jesus, direct our way to you; [12] and may the Lord make you increase and abound in love to one another and to all men, as we do to you, [13] so that he may establish your hearts unblamable in holiness before our God and Father, at the coming of our Lord Jesus with all his saints.

Pray the following prayer together as a group.

In the name of the Father, and of the Son,
and of the Holy Spirit. Amen.

Lord,
We thank you for calling this group together. Teach us to care for each other the way St. Paul cared for the Thessalonians. Through your care, clear the way for us to grow closer to you over the next six weeks. Increase our love, strengthen our hearts, and make us blameless and holy as we earnestly seek to live in your presence. We pray this through Christ our Lord. Amen.

Introduction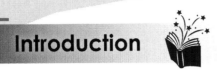

"If you have not already read the introduction to this study, please find time during this next week to read through it. It will provide you with some helpful background information on St. Paul as well as the spirituality of this study."

Read aloud.
The meaning of love is something that has fascinated generations of artists and scholars alike. Because our love is imperfect, we are often frustrated and confused by it. St. Paul's life was one of fierce love and intensity. The imperfection of his love drove him to persecute the followers of Jesus. God's perfect love rescued Saul from this dead-end road and made him a blessing for the entire world. St. Paul's love of Jesus led him to endure the most terrible conditions, establish vital churches across the Greco-Roman empire, and in the end to die a martyr's death. We may continue to struggle with the experience of human love in our lives. However, as we study the life of St. Paul this week, we will get a clearer picture of and truly experience the love of God...the love that moves mountains...the love that God wishes to lavish on us all.

Paul's Life and Mission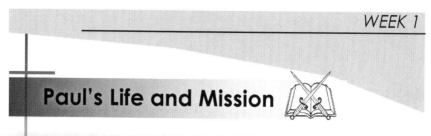

Have someone read the following passage aloud.

Acts 9:1-20

[1]Meanwhile, Saul was still breathing out murderous threats against the Lord's disciples. He went to the high priest [2]and asked him for letters to the synagogues in Damascus, so that if he found any there who belonged to the Way, whether men or women, he might take them as prisoners to Jerusalem. [3]As he neared Damascus on his journey, suddenly a light from heaven flashed around him. [4]He fell to the ground and heard a voice say to him, "Saul, Saul, why do you persecute me?"

[5]"Who are you, Lord?" Saul asked.

"I am Jesus, whom you are persecuting," he replied. [6]"Now get up and go into the city, and you will be told what you must do."

[7]The men traveling with Saul stood there speechless; they heard the sound but did not see anyone. [8]Saul got up from the ground, but when he opened his eyes he could see nothing. So they led him by the hand into Damascus. [9]For three days he was blind, and did not eat or drink anything.

[10]In Damascus there was a disciple named Ananias. The Lord called to him in a vision, "Ananias!"
"Yes, Lord," he answered.

[11]The Lord told him, "Go to the house of Judas on Straight Street and ask for a man from Tarsus named Saul, for he is praying. [12]In a vision he has seen a man named Ananias come and place his hands on him to restore his sight."

16

[13]"Lord," Ananias answered, "I have heard many reports about this man and all the harm he has done to your saints in Jerusalem. [14]And he has come here with authority from the chief priests to arrest all who call on your name."

[15]But the Lord said to Ananias, "Go! This man is my chosen instrument to carry my name before the Gentiles and their kings and before the people of Israel. [16]I will show him how much he must suffer for my name."

[17]Then Ananias went to the house and entered it. Placing his hands on Saul, he said, "Brother Saul, the Lord—Jesus, who appeared to you on the road as you were coming here—has sent me so that you may see again and be filled with the Holy Spirit." [18]Immediately, something like scales fell from Saul's eyes, and he could see again. He got up and was baptized, [19]and after taking some food, he regained his strength. Saul spent several days with the disciples in Damascus. [20]At once he began to preach in the synagogues that Jesus is the Son of God.

1. Based on Saul's actions, how do you think he would describe the God he was serving? How do you think he would describe Jesus after the revelation? After his three day wait to have his sight restored?

2. What do you think motivated Ananias to obey Jesus when Jesus told him what to do?

3. This passage is often titled, "Saul's Conversion." Christians use various phrases to describe their understanding of conversion, such as "saved," "baptized," "received Christ," "repented," "changed," "reconciled," or "renewed." Which of these would you say best describes Saul's conversion? How do you feel about these terms?

4. Have you had an experience of God that might be described by one of these words? Would you be willing to share your experience?

Holy Scripture

Have someone read the following passage aloud.

Romans 8:28-39

[28]We know that in everything God works for good with those who love him, who are called according to his purpose. [29]For those whom he foreknew he also predestined to be conformed to the image of his Son, in order that he might be the first-born among many brethren. [30]And those whom he predestined he also called; and those whom he called he also justified; and those whom he justified he also glorified. [31]What then shall we say to this? If God is for us, who is against us? [32]He who did not spare his own Son but gave him up for us all, will he not also give us all things with him? [33]Who shall bring any charge against God's elect? It is God who justifies; [34]who is to condemn? Is it Christ Jesus, who died, yes, who was raised from the dead, who is at the right hand of God, who indeed intercedes for us? [35]Who shall separate us from the love of Christ? Shall tribulation, or distress, or persecution, or famine, or nakedness, or peril, or sword? [36]As it is written, "For thy sake we are being killed all the day long; we are regarded as sheep to be slaughtered." [37]No, in all these things we are more than conquerors through him who loved us. [38]For I am sure that neither death, nor life, nor angels, nor principalities, nor things present, nor things to come, nor powers, [39]nor height, nor depth, nor anything else in all creation, will be able to separate us from the love of God in Christ Jesus our Lord.

5. How would you define love?

6. When do you feel the most loved?

7. How would you put v.28 in your own words? Discuss the different versions offered by group members and why some prefer one meaning over the other.

8. Verses 29 and 30 give several verbs describing God's action toward those who love him. What are some of these verbs? What do they tell you about God's intentions toward you?

9. How do verses 31 and 32 fit with your thoughts about God's intentions in verses 29-30?

10. What threats to realizing God's intentions toward us does Paul address in verses 35-39? Have you experienced any of these in your life? How? When?

11. What part of this passage is the most meaningful to you?

"Do you love me because I'm beautiful, or am I beautiful because you love me?"

-Oscar Hammerstein, II

Have someone read the following passage aloud.

Ephesians 2:3-9

[3]Among these we all once lived in the passions of our flesh, following the desires of body and mind, and so we were by nature children of wrath, like the rest of mankind. [4]But God, who is rich in mercy, out of the great love with which he loved us, [5]even when we were dead through our trespasses, made us alive together with Christ (by grace you have been saved), [6]and raised us up with him, and made us sit with him in the heavenly places in Christ Jesus, [7]that in the coming ages he might show the immeasurable riches of his grace in kindness toward us in Christ Jesus. [8]For by grace you have been saved through faith; and this is not your own doing, it is the gift of God -- [9]not because of works, lest any man should boast.

12. What do you think it means to be "dead through our trespasses?"

13. How would you define the word "grace?" [1]

14. What could this passage offer to someone who felt like they had to get their life back in order before opening their life back up to God?

15. Many different phrases in this passage reveal God's love and blessings toward us. What phrase is the most significant to you? Why?

(If you have time, the Appendix contains two paragraphs from the <u>Catechism of the Catholic Church</u> *about God's love that you could read and reflect on together as a group.)*

---

[1]Fr. Harden's *Pocket Catholic Dictionary* defines grace as, "the unmerited gift proceeding from th[e] benevolent disposition [of God]. p.166.

Your Life and Mission

• Read the daily readings this week and look for specific examples of where God's love is shown—perhaps record them in a journal. Also, look for specific ways God shows His love for you daily, and record those also. On Sunday morning, review God's blessings shown to you through the week and praise Him for them at Mass.

• When the opportunity arises, boast of God's love to 3 people during this week. Use your reflections on these Scriptures and your own life as a guide.

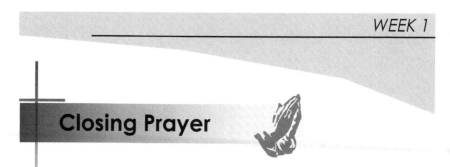

Closing Prayer

The facilitator could ask for any prayer petitions that people have. The group could spend time praying for each other—perhaps everyone praying for the person on their right. Then pray the Closing Prayer based on Ephesians 3:14-21 aloud together.

In the name of the Father, and of the Son, and of the Holy Spirit. Amen. [Prayer for any petitions.]

Father in heaven, help us to"know the love of Christ which surpasses knowledge." Give us the power to comprehend how wide and long, how high and deep His love is for us. We open ourselves to your great power, which is at work in us to do far more than we can ask or imagine. Thank you for this time together and for St. Paul's witness to your love.

[Facilitator]: St. Paul
[Group members]: Pray for us.

In the name of the Father, and of the Son, and of the Holy Spirit. Amen.

TEMPTATION

WEEK 2

"My grace is sufficient for you, for my power is made perfect in weakness"

2 Corinthians 12:9

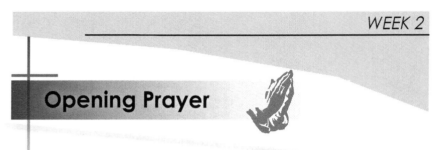

Opening Prayer

Have someone read the following passage aloud.

1 Corinthians 1:1-9

[1]Paul, called by the will of God to be an apostle of Christ Jesus, and our brother Sos'thenes, [2]To the church of God which is at Corinth, to those sanctified in Christ Jesus, called to be saints together with all those who in every place call on the name of our Lord Jesus Christ, both their Lord and ours: [3]Grace to you and peace from God our Father and the Lord Jesus Christ. [4]I give thanks to God always for you because of the grace of God which was given you in Christ Jesus, [5]that in every way you were enriched in him with all speech and all knowledge -- [6]even as the testimony to Christ was confirmed among you -- [7]so that you are not lacking in any spiritual gift, as you wait for the revealing of our Lord Jesus Christ; [8]who will sustain you to the end, guiltless in the day of our Lord Jesus Christ. [9]God is faithful, by whom you were called into the fellowship of his Son, Jesus Christ our Lord.

Pray together:

In the name of the Father, and of the Son, and of the Holy Spirit. Amen.

Almighty God, we long to claim and use the spiritual gifts that help us to live guiltlessly, from love instead of fear. Help us to become aware of the gifts you want to give to us. Strengthen us through them for the battles we fight in our own lives. We ask these things through Jesus our Lord, who himself was tempted in every way we are, yet lived a life in perfect union with your will. AMEN.

Introduction

Have someone read the following aloud.

All of us will be tempted to live a life contrary to the life God has freely offered us through his Son, our Lord Jesus Christ. The battle with sin is not one we can merely wish away. We must get in the fight to live holy lives. Even St. Paul had to wrestle with temptation.

Holy Scripture

Have someone read the following passage aloud.

2 Corinthians 12:2-10

[2]I know a man in Christ who fourteen years ago was caught up to the third heaven -- whether in the body or out of the body I do not know, God knows. [3]And I know that this man was caught up into Paradise -- whether in the body or out of the body I do not know, God knows -- [4]and he heard things that cannot be told, which man may not utter. [5]On behalf of this man I will boast, but on my own behalf I will not boast, except of my weaknesses. [6]Though if I wish to boast, I shall not be a fool, for I shall be speaking the truth. But I refrain from it, so that no one may think more of me than he sees in me or hears from me. [7]And to keep me from being too elated by the abundance of revelations, a thorn was given me in the flesh, a messenger of Satan, to harass me, to keep me from being too elated. [8]Three times I besought the Lord about this, that it should leave me; [9]but he said to me, "My grace is sufficient for you, for my power is made perfect in weakness." I will all the more gladly boast of my weaknesses, that the power of Christ may rest upon me. [10]For the sake of Christ, then, I am content with weaknesses, insults, hardships, persecutions, and calamities; for when I am weak, then I am strong.

1. Looking back, can you recall a particular "thorn in your side?" Why was it a "thorn?"

2. What did you learn from your struggles? Did you see any fruit produced from your difficulties, or do you still see those struggles as purely negative experiences?

3. In this passage, St. Paul says the thorn is "a messenger from Satan." What message do you think the thorn bears?

4. How do you react to the idea of a "messenger from Satan?" Do you ever think about your struggles and temptations as a battle with "the evil one" (Jesus taught us in the "Our Father" to pray: "Deliver us from the evil one." That is the literal translation from the Greek of the Lord's prayer.)

5. What does God promise to St. Paul in verse 9? What do you think might have been Paul's reaction to God's response?

6. Do you feel like God's grace has been sufficient for you in your own struggles and temptations?

7. Can you think of times in your life where you have witnessed weakness being turned into strength through the power of God?

8. Do you think it is possible to "delight" in your own weakness (verse 10)? How might that be possible? How does this relate to our temptations?

Read the following aloud.

Ephesians 6:10-20

[10]Finally, be strong in the Lord and in the strength of his might. [11]Put on the whole armor of God, that you may be able to stand against the wiles of the devil. [12]For we are not contending against flesh and blood, but against the principalities, against the powers, against the world rulers of this present darkness, against the spiritual hosts of wickedness in the heavenly places. [13]Therefore take the whole armor of God, that you may be able to withstand in the evil day, and having done all, to

stand. [14]Stand therefore, having girded your loins with truth, and having put on the breastplate of righteousness, [15]and having shod your feet with the equipment of the gospel of peace; [16]besides all these, taking the shield of faith, with which you can quench all the flaming darts of the evil one. [17]And take the helmet of salvation, and the sword of the Spirit, which is the word of God. [18]Pray at all times in the Spirit, with all prayer and supplication. To that end keep alert with all perseverance, making supplication for all the saints, [19]and also for me, that utterance may be given me in opening my mouth boldly to proclaim the mystery of the gospel, [20]for which I am an ambassador in chains; that I may declare it boldly, as I ought to speak.

9. Military analogies for the spiritual life are not uncommon in the Bible, or in our Catholic spiritual tradition. How do you react to St. Paul's use of it here? Do you find it inspiring, off-putting, confusing, apt?

10. Verse 11 states that our armor will help us "to stand against the wiles of the devil" Verse 12 describes our enemies in the struggle. How do you think these forces are attacking us? What are they trying to accomplish? How do they relate to our struggle against temptation?

11. What are the different pieces of God's armor outlined in this passage? Which piece or pieces of God's armor do you feel you utilize most effectively, and which pieces would you like to utilize and cooperate with better in your life? Explain.

12. Do you feel that you have "the word of God" available to you as a sword of the spirit? What would it look like to draw on it when engaged in spiritual battle? How could it be more readily at hand?

13. Verse 18 seems to set a very high bar for prayer. What are some ways Catholics could apply verse 18 in our lives today? How does the text show how this relates to our battle with temptation?

Your Life and Mission

- Set aside times for prayer this week to reflect more on the armor of God. Read back over 1 Corinthians 1 and Ephesians 6 to examine areas in your life that are either thorns or susceptible to attack. What are your areas of temptation? What is God teaching you through this fight against temptation? What can you do to put on God's armor and resist temptation in order to serve the Lord faithfully?

- Consider going to confession this week after making a thorough examination of conscience. Pray for eyes to see, ears to hear, and a heart to feel the sufficiency of God's grace in your life and invite the Holy Spirit to live fully in you. Confess any times that you have given into temptation. You might also confess a realization that you are feeling increasingly weak in the face of temptation. The Sacrament will strengthen your resolve against sin and clothe you again with God's armor. (See Appendix)

- Pray through Romans 7:21 - 8:11 on your own and notice how it flows into the passage we studied last week from Romans 8 on God's love. What is the overarching point Paul is teaching?

Closing Prayer

Allow the group to pray silently for a few moments about the temptations they have faced or know they will face soon. Then, pray the following exhortation aloud together.

1 Timothy 6:11-16

[11]But you, man of God, flee from all this, and pursue righteousness, godliness, faith, love, endurance and gentleness. [12]Fight the good fight of the faith. Take hold of the eternal life to which you were called when you made your good confession in the presence of many witnesses. [13]In the sight of God, who gives life to everything, and of Christ Jesus, who while testifying before Pontius Pilate made the good confession, I charge you [14]to keep this command without spot or blame until the appearing of our Lord Jesus Christ, [15]which God will bring about in his own time—God, the blessed and only Ruler, the King of kings and Lord of lords, [16]who alone is immortal and who lives in unapproachable light, whom no one has seen or can see. To him be honor and might forever. Amen.

[Facilitator]: St. Paul

[Group members]: Pray for us.

VIRTUE

WEEK 3

*"Those who belong to Christ Jesus
have crucified the flesh
with its passions and desires"*

Galatians 5:24

Opening Prayer

Have someone read the following passage of Scripture and the following prayer aloud for our opening prayer.

Colossians 1:1-6

[1]Paul, an apostle of Christ Jesus by the will of God, and Timothy our brother, [2]To the saints and faithful brethren in Christ at Colos'sae: Grace to you and peace from God our Father. [3]We always thank God, the Father of our Lord Jesus Christ, when we pray for you, [4]because we have heard of your faith in Christ Jesus and of the love which you have for all the saints, [5]because of the hope laid up for you in heaven. Of this you have heard before in the word of the truth, the gospel [6]which has come to you, as indeed in the whole world it is bearing fruit and growing -- so among yourselves, from the day you heard and understood the grace of God in truth,

In the name of the Father, and of the Son, and of the Holy Spirit. Amen.

Dear God, We ask for the grace to become like the Colossians. Build up our faith through our conversation. Help us to love one another and our neighbor so that all will know the good fruit borne from life in Christ Jesus. Help us to nurture the hope you offer in Christ through an intimate relationship with Him in prayer and sacrament. Allow us to be touched and changed by Paul's example and teaching about the way a follower of Christ should live. Make us a people of hope. We ask these things through Jesus Christ our Lord, who lives and reigns with you for ever and ever. AMEN.

Introduction

Read aloud:

At the time St. Paul wrote, the word "saints" didn't refer to those who had been officially beatified or canonized. No such procedure yet existed. St. Paul used the word "saints" to refer to all Christians. The Greek word is also sometimes translated as "holy ones."

Paul's Life and Mission

Have someone read the following passage aloud.

Paul's Life and Mission: Acts 16:16-34, set in Philippi

[16]As we were going to the place of prayer, we were met by a slave girl who had a spirit of divination and brought her owners much gain by soothsaying. [17]She followed Paul and us, crying, "These men are servants of the Most High God, who proclaim to you the way of salvation." [18]And this she did for many days. But Paul was annoyed, and turned and said to the spirit, "I charge you in the name of Jesus Christ to come out of her." And it came out that very hour. [19]But when her owners saw that their hope of gain was gone, they seized Paul and Silas and dragged them into the market place before the rulers; [20]and when they had brought them to the magistrates they said, "These men are Jews and they are disturbing our city. [21]They advocate customs which it is not lawful for us Romans to accept or practice." [22]The crowd joined in attacking them; and the magistrates tore the garments off them and gave orders to beat them with rods. [23]And when they had inflicted many blows upon them, they threw them into prison, charging the jailer to keep them safely. [24]Having received this charge, he put them into the inner prison and fastened their feet in the stocks. [25]But about

35

midnight Paul and Silas were praying and singing hymns to God, and the prisoners were listening to them, [26]and suddenly there was a great earthquake, so that the foundations of the prison were shaken; and immediately all the doors were opened and every one's fetters were unfastened. [27]When the jailer woke and saw that the prison doors were open, he drew his sword and was about to kill himself, supposing that the prisoners had escaped. [28]But Paul cried with a loud voice, "Do not harm yourself, for we are all here." [29]And he called for lights and rushed in, and trembling with fear he fell down before Paul and Silas, [30]and brought them out and said, "Men, what must I do to be saved?" [31]And they said, "Believe in the Lord Jesus, and you will be saved, you and your household." [32]And they spoke the word of the Lord to him and to all that were in his house. [33]And he took them the same hour of the night, and washed their wounds, and he was baptized at once, with all his family. [34]Then he brought them up into his house, and set food before them; and he rejoiced with all his household that he had believed in God.

1. Have you ever wanted desperately to know what will happen in the future? What was happening in your life? Why did you want to know so badly?

2. In the Opening Prayer from the book of Colossians, St. Paul commended the Colossians for their faith, hope and love. Which of these virtues do you think Paul and Silas were primarily exercising as they prayed and sang hymns in prison?

3. What would you do to nurture faith, hope, and love in such a situation?

4. Why do you think Paul and Silas remained in prison when they could have escaped?

5. In your own life, what interferes with the kind of faith and trust in God Paul and Silas showed?

6. Why do you think the jailer after discovering them would immediately ask Paul and Silas how to be saved? What do you think he saw in Paul and Silas that he wanted for himself?

7. The jailer rejoices as he feeds Paul and Silas, because he, with his whole family, had come to believe in God. Does your faith in God bring you joy?

8. The meal they share could be an allusion to the Eucharist. Does the Eucharist bring you joy? Do you have any practices that help deepen your experience of the sacrament?

Holy Scripture

Have someone read the following passage aloud.

Galatians 5:1, 13-26

[1]For freedom Christ has set us free; stand fast therefore, and do not submit again to a yoke of slavery.

[13]For you were called to freedom, brethren; only do not use your freedom as an opportunity for the flesh, but through love be servants of one another. [14]For the whole law is fulfilled in one word, "You shall love your neighbor as yourself." [15]But if you bite and devour one another take heed that you are not consumed by one another. [16]But I say, walk by the Spirit, and do not gratify the desires of the flesh. [17]For the desires of the flesh are against the Spirit, and the desires of the Spirit are against the flesh; for these are opposed to each other, to prevent you from doing what you would. [18]But if you are led by the Spirit you are not under the law. [19]Now the works of the flesh are plain: fornication, impurity, licentiousness, [20]idolatry, sorcery, enmity, strife, jealousy, anger, selfishness, dissension, party spirit, [21]envy, drunkenness, carousing, and the like. I warn you, as I warned you before, that those who do such things shall not inherit the kingdom of God. [22]But the fruit of the Spirit is love, joy, peace, patience, kindness, goodness, faithfulness, [23]gentleness, self-control; against such there is no law. [24]And those who belong to Christ Jesus have crucified the flesh with its passions and desires. [25]If we live by the Spirit, let us also walk by the Spirit. [26]Let us have no self-conceit, no provoking of one another, no envy of one another.

9. What does it mean to be free? Given the rest of the passage we read, what kind of freedom do you think Paul has in mind?

10. How do you understand Paul's negative use of the term "the flesh?"

11. How would you define the word "fruit?" Paul describes things contrary to God as "works of the flesh." Why do you think Paul uses the phrase "fruit of the spirit" instead of "works of the spirit?"

12. Were there qualities that surprised you in either of the lists, the works of the flesh and the fruits of the Spirit?

13. Assuming the Galatians weren't literally chomping on one another, what do you think St. Paul meant by this metaphor? In what ways do we bite and devour one another now?

14. Jesus says that we must love not just those who love us, but also our enemies. How can that even be possible? Have you had a time when you tried to love someone who wronged you? How did you go about it? Was there anything that helped? Anything that hindered?

15. This passage tells us we can walk by the Spirit (v.16, 25), be led by the Spirit (v.18), and live by the Spirit (v.25). How do we do that in our daily lives?

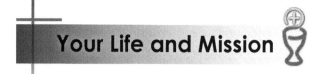

Your Life and Mission

• When you lack joy and peace, patience and kindness, gentleness and self-control, do you look to see in what ways you are living "from the flesh" as a cause of these weaknesses? Plan some way this week to seek connections between your actions and your inner life either using the Galatians reading, or the Examen below.

• Meditate this week on the "yoke of slavery" in your life. Ask Christ to make that yoke easy, that burden light. Then follow up by repeating in prayer, aloud or to yourself: "For freedom Christ has set me free." Repeat it as many times as you like…. It's the good news!

• St. Paul's lists of the fruits of the flesh and the Spirit have long been an extremely important tool for Christians seeking to live more fully as a follower of Jesus. St. Ignatius of Loyola, the founder of the Jesuits, used this passage in his Spiritual Exercises as a tool of discernment. By looking at the fruits in your life, and seeking correlations between your inner life and your acts, you can discern what keeps you bound, and what sets you free. To help people do that, St. Ignatius developed a prayer process known as "the Examen." (Pronounced ex Ā men) Try this method of prayer this week.

A modern version of the Examen of St. Ignatius of Loyola

• We begin the Examen with an awareness of God's presence with us and ask for the guidance of the Holy Spirit to prayerfully reflect on our day/week.

• We reflect on our day/week and ask ourselves how God has been present in the events of our day and in the feelings we experienced that day.

• We then look at how Christ has called us through these experiences as well as how we responded to these calls.

• Another helpful method for the Examen is to look at what we are grateful for and what has given us life this day. And then look, on the other hand, at what we are not so grateful for and what has drained life from us.

• We thank God for the blessings of the day.

• We also beg God's forgiveness for any failures to respond well to Christ's calls that day.

• We end by asking God's help to respond generously to Christ's calls to us during the coming day.

Closing Prayer

Invite members of the group to offer prayers of petition or thanksgiving. Then invite them to read aloud the closing prayer together, which is based upon Romans 12:1-2.

In the name of the Father, and of the Son, and of the Holy Spirit. Amen.

[Prayers of petition or thanksgiving]

Lord, this week we ask that you would give us grace to live lives that are holy and acceptable to you. Renew our minds so that we will know your good, acceptable, and perfect will. We pray this through Christ our Lord. Amen.

[Facilitator]: St. Paul

[Group members]: Pray for us.

SUFFERING

WEEK 4

"While we live we are always being given up to death for Jesus' sake, so that the life of Jesus may be manifested in our mortal flesh."

2 Corinthians 4:11

Opening Prayer

Have someone read the following passage.

2 Corinthians 1:1-7.

1Paul, an apostle of Christ Jesus by the will of God, and Timothy our brother. To the church of God which is at Corinth, with all the saints who are in the whole of Acha'ia: 2Grace to you and peace from God our Father and the Lord Jesus Christ. 3Blessed be the God and Father of our Lord Jesus Christ, the Father of mercies and God of all comfort, 4who comforts us in all our affliction, so that we may be able to comfort those who are in any affliction, with the comfort with which we ourselves are comforted by God. 5For as we share abundantly in Christ's sufferings, so through Christ we share abundantly in comfort too. 6If we are afflicted, it is for your comfort and salvation; and if we are comforted, it is for your comfort, which you experience when you patiently endure the same sufferings that we suffer. 7Our hope for you is unshaken; for we know that as you share in our sufferings, you will also share in our comfort.

Pray the following aloud together.
In the name of the Father, and of the Son, and of the Holy Spirit. Amen.

Dear Lord. We all face troubles and challenges in our lives, sometimes very difficult ones. Our hope fails. We are tempted to despair. Yet we know that your Son suffered too, because of your love for us. Help us bind our suffering to His. We pray for comfort and consolation. Let our troubles produce patient endurance, not despair. Through our pain, make us more compassionate to the suffering of others. We ask these things through Christ our Lord, whose passion and resurrection brought us salvation. Amen.

Paul's Life and Mission

Have someone read the following passage aloud.

Acts 14: 8 – 22

[8]Now at Lystra there was a man sitting, who could not use his feet; he was a cripple from birth, who had never walked. [9]He listened to Paul speaking; and Paul, looking intently at him and seeing that he had faith to be made well, [10]said in a loud voice, "Stand upright on your feet." And he sprang up and walked. [11]And when the crowds saw what Paul had done, they lifted up their voices, saying in Lycao'nian, "The gods have come down to us in the likeness of men!" [12]Barnabas they called Zeus, and Paul, because he was the chief speaker, they called Hermes. [13]And the priest of Zeus, whose temple was in front of the city, brought oxen and garlands to the gates and wanted to offer sacrifice with the people. [14]But when the apostles Barnabas and Paul heard of it, they tore their garments and rushed out among the multitude, crying, [15]"Men, why are you doing this? We also are men, of like nature with you, and bring you good news, that you should turn from these vain things to a living God who made the heaven and the earth and the sea and all that is in them. [16]In past generations he allowed all the nations to walk in their own ways; [17]yet he did not leave himself without witness, for he did good and gave you from heaven rains and fruitful seasons, satisfying your hearts with food and gladness." [18]With these words they scarcely restrained the people from offering sacrifice to them. [19]But Jews came there from Antioch and Ico'nium; and having persuaded the people, they stoned Paul and dragged him out of the city, supposing that he was dead. [20]But when the disciples gathered about him, he rose up and entered the city; and on the next day he went on with Barnabas to Derbe. [21]When they had preached the gospel to that city and had made many disciples, they returned to Lystra and

to Ico'nium and to Antioch, [22]strengthening the souls of the disciples, exhorting them to continue in the faith, and saying that through many tribulations we must enter the kingdom of God.

1. How would you explain the change in the crowd's treatment of St. Paul and Barnabas from the beginning to the end of the story? How do you think St. Paul felt about it? Contrast St. Paul's response to adversity with your own. What can you learn from him?

Holy Scripture

Have someone read the following passage aloud.

Romans 5:2-5

[2]Through him we have obtained access to this grace in which we stand, and we rejoice in our hope of sharing the glory of God. [3]More than that, we rejoice in our sufferings, knowing that suffering produces endurance, [4]and endurance produces character, and character produces hope, [5]and hope does not disappoint us, because God's love has been poured into our hearts through the Holy Spirit which has been given to us.

2. Why does Paul say he rejoices in his sufferings?

3. Why would endurance lead to character?

4. Have you had an experience when you felt you were able to practice endurance through suffering in your own life, or have you seen it in someone else? What kind of character does it require? Can it lead to hopefulness?

5. Below is an excerpt from Pope Benedict XVI's second encyclical, Spe Salvi. Read it together and discuss how this passage relates to our passage from Romans. How do these teachings on hope relate to your life?

From Pope Benedict XVI's Spe Salvi:

"[Paul] says to the Thessalonians: you must not "grieve as others do who have no hope" (1 Th 4:13). Here too we see as a distinguishing mark of Christians the fact that they have a future: it is not that they know the details of what awaits them, but they know in general terms that their life will not end in emptiness. Only when the future is certain as a positive reality does it become possible to live the present as well. So now we can say: Christianity was not only "good news"—the communication of a hitherto unknown content. In our language we would say: the Christian message was not only "informative" but "performative". That means: the Gospel is not merely a communication of things that can be known—it is one that makes things happen and is life-changing. The dark door of time, of the future, has been thrown open. The one who has hope lives differently; the one who hopes has been granted the gift of a new life."[2]

Have someone read the following passage aloud.

2 Corinthians 4:5-12, 16-18

[5]For what we preach is not ourselves, but Jesus Christ as Lord, with ourselves as your servants for Jesus' sake. [6]For it is the God who said, "Let light shine out of darkness," who has shone in our hearts to give the light of the knowledge of the glory of God in the face of Christ. [7]But we have this treasure in earthen vessels, to show that the transcendent power belongs to God and not to us. [8]We are afflicted in every way, but not crushed; perplexed, but not driven to despair; [9]persecuted, but not forsaken; struck down, but not destroyed; [10]always carrying in the body the death of Jesus, so that the life of Jesus may also be manifested in our bodies. [11]For while we live we are always being given up to death for Jesus' sake, so that the life of Jesus may be manifested in our mortal flesh. [12]So death is at work in us, but life in you.

[16]So we do not lose heart. Though our outer nature is wasting away, our inner nature is being renewed every day. [17]For this slight mometary

---

[2] Pope Benedict XVI, Spe Salvi (November 30, 2007)

affliction is preparing for us an eternal weight of glory beyond all comparison, [18]because we look not to the things that are seen but to the things that are unseen; for the things that are seen are transient, but the things that are unseen are eternal.

6. This is one of the most famous passages in the epistles on suffering. What stands out for you? What do you find appealing, off-putting, or consoling and why?

7. In verse 7, what is the treasure Paul is referring to? What are the earthen vessels?

8. Verses 8 and 9 describe different types of suffering. Which of these can you most identify with?

9. Verse 10 identifies these sufferings with the body of Jesus. Did you ever think of your suffering as identifying with His suffering? Or that Jesus identifies with your suffering? What does that mean to you?

10. There are many promises listed here for those who suffer. Which one(s) particularly strike you?

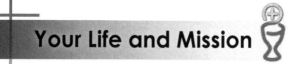

Your Life and Mission

In the Spiritual Exercises, St. Ignatius Loyola, the founder of the Jesuits wrote "the First Principle and Foundation." Here is a modern paraphrase by David L. Fleming, SJ.

Have one person read this aloud.

The goal of our life is to live with God forever.
God, who loves us, gave us life.
Our own response of love allows God's life

To flow into us without limit.
All the things in this world are gifts of God,
Presented to us so that we can know God more easily
And make a return of love more readily.

As a result, we appreciate and use all these gifts of God
Insofar as they help us develop as loving persons.
But if any of these gifts become the center of our lives,
They displace God
And so hinder our growth toward our goal.

In everyday life, then, we must hold ourselves in balance
before all of these created gifts insofar as we have a choice
and are not bound by some obligation.
We should not fix our desires on health or sickness,
wealth or poverty, success or failure, a long life or short one.
For everything has the potential of calling forth in us
a deeper response to our life in God.

Our only desire and our one choice should be this:
I want and I choose what better leads
to God's deepening God's life in me.

*Try praying this prayer at least three times this week, especially when
you are suffering.*

Closing Prayer

For the closing prayer, share whatever personal petitions you might have and offer prayers for each other in whatever way is comfortable. Close with the prayer below, based on Ephesians 1:16-23.

In the name of the Father, and of the Son, and of the Holy Spirit. Amen.

Father of glory, give us a spirit of wisdom and revelation in the knowledge of your son Jesus, enlighten the eyes of our hearts to know the hope to which you have called us in baptism, the glorious inheritance we have with the saints, and the immeasurable power that you offer us in Jesus' name.

We ask these things through Jesus Christ our Lord, who lives and reigns with you for ever and ever. Amen.

[Facilitator]: St. Paul

[Group members]: Pray for us.

SPIRIT

WEEK 5

"If the Spirit of him who raised Jesus from the dead dwells in you, he who raised Christ Jesus from the dead will give life to your mortal bodies."

Romans 8:11

Opening Prayer

Have someone read the following passage of Scripture aloud for our opening prayer.

2 Corinthians 1:21-22

[21]But it is God who establishes us with you in Christ, and has commissioned us; [22]he has put his seal upon us and given us his Spirit in our hearts as a guarantee.

In the name of the Father, and of the Son, and of the Holy Spirit. Amen.

Our Father in heaven, we don't want to miss out on any dimension of the new life you offer us in baptism. It is you who establishes us in Christ. It is you who has commissioned us and put your seal of ownership upon us. Open our eyes to the workings of your Holy Spirit in our lives and to your desire to continually fill us. Holy Spirit, fill our hearts. We ask this through Christ our Lord. Amen.

Introduction

The Holy Spirit has been called the neglected member of the Trinity. We believe that the Holy Spirit is co-equal with the Father and the Son. We believe he is "the Lord, the giver of life." These are powerful attributes indeed. We also believe that the Holy Spirit is the one throughout the ages that has "spoken through the prophets."

So many times in our life we might begin signing ourselves by reverently saying, "In the name of the Father and of the Son," but by the time we get to the Holy Spirit our minds are already on to the meal

54

sitting before us or to our next task for that day. Even during focused times of prayer, it might be easy for us to remember the Father when we are asking for help – or Jesus when we look at a crucifix – but when is the last time you thought about the Holy Spirit in your life?

The Holy Spirit was clearly more than a passing thought for St. Paul. This week we examine some of the passages of Scripture in which Paul demonstrates the importance of the Holy Spirit in our lives.

Paul's Life and Mission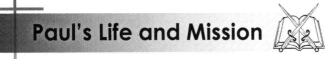

Acts 18:2 - 19:7

[22]When he had landed at Caesare'a, he went up and greeted the church, and then went down to Antioch. [23]After spending some time there he departed and went from place to place through the region of Galatia and Phryg'ia, strengthening all the disciples. [24]Now a Jew named Apol'los, a native of Alexandria, came to Ephesus. He was an eloquent man, well versed in the scriptures. [25]He had been instructed in the way of the Lord; and being fervent in spirit, he spoke and taught accurately the things concerning Jesus, though he knew only the baptism of John. [26]He began to speak boldly in the synagogue; but when Priscilla and Aq'uila heard him, they took him and expounded to him the way of God more accurately. [27]And when he wished to cross to Acha'ia, the brethren encouraged him, and wrote to the disciples to receive him. When he arrived, he greatly helped those who through grace had believed, [28]for he powerfully confuted the Jews in public, showing by the scriptures that the Christ was Jesus.

[1]While Apol'los was at Corinth, Paul passed through the upper country and came to Ephesus. There he found some disciples. [2]And he said to them, "Did you receive the Holy Spirit when you believed?" And they said, "No, we have never even heard that there is a Holy Spirit." [3]And he said, "Into what then were you baptized?" They said, "Into John's

baptism." [4]And Paul said, "John baptized with the baptism of repentance, telling the people to believe in the one who was to come after him, that is, Jesus." [5]On hearing this, they were baptized in the name of the Lord Jesus. [6]And when Paul had laid his hands upon them, the Holy Spirit came on them; and they spoke with tongues [3] and prophesied. [7]There were about twelve of them in all.

1. Apollos spoke with "burning enthusiasm" and with accuracy regarding Jesus, but Priscilla and Aquila picked up on certain things that were a bit off in his teaching. Have you ever had this experience when listening to someone talk about Christianity?

2. How do you think Apollos reacted to Priscilla and Aquila's teaching?

3. Apollos had been preaching in Ephesus when Priscilla and Aquila instructed him more accurately. When Paul arrives in Ephesus after Apollos had left, he finds some disciples. What do these disciples have in common with Apollos?

4. What differences were there between Priscilla and Aquila's effect on Apollos and Paul's effect on the Ephesian disciples? In the text, what was different about these interactions? How much would you attribute to Paul's authority or "office" among the disciples?

Please read aloud the following passage.

Some people in Christianity, including some Catholics, follow certain passages in Acts and speak of a "Baptism of the Spirit." This is being filled with the Holy Spirit after one's baptism. This is confusing to some, but also a reality that leads many people to a deeper relationship with Christ and the Church. Please read aloud the following excerpts from the preaching of Fr. Raniero Cantalamessa, OFM, Papal preacher to Pope John Paul II:

"What does it mean to say that Jesus is he who baptizes with the Holy

---

[3] Please see Appendix E for more on this in the Catechism of the Catholic Church

Spirit? The expression serves not only to distinguish Jesus' baptism from John's baptism; it serves to distinguish the entire person and work of Christ from that of the precursor. In other words, in all of his work Jesus is the one who baptizes in the Holy Spirit," he said. "The Risen Jesus baptizes in the Spirit not only in the sacrament of baptism, but, in a different way, also in other moments: in the Eucharist, in listening to the Word and, in general, through all the channels of grace." [4]

"The Baptism in the Spirit is not a sacrament, but it is related to several sacraments. The Baptism in the Spirit makes real and in a way renews Christian initiation. At the beginning of the Church, Baptism was administered to adults who converted from paganism and who, made on the occasion of Baptism, an act of faith and a free and mature choice. Today...[with infant baptism] rarely, or never, does the baptized person ever reach the stage of proclaiming in the Holy Spirit "Jesus is Lord". And until one reaches this point, everything else in the Christian life remains out of focus and immature...The Baptism in the Spirit effectiveness in reactivating baptism consists in this: finally man contributes his part - namely, he makes a choice of faith, prepared in repentance that allows the work of God to set itself free and to emanate all its strength. It is as if the plug is pulled and the light is switched on. The gift of God is finally "untied" and the Spirit is allowed to flow like a fragrance in the Christian life." [5]

5. What does Fr. Cantalamessa say is the Baptism in the Spirit? How is it related to a person's Baptism?

6. What is the effect of this light being switched on in a baptized person's life?

---

[4] Father Raniero Cantalamessa, OFM, quoted in 12/14/2007 Zenit article entitled, "Preacher Sees Holy Spirit as Therapy." Available at http://www.catholic.net/index. php?option=dedestaca&id=111&category=Life%20&%20Family~Marriage.
[5] Cantalamessa, OFM, "The Baptism of the Holy Spirit," Originally from the (ICCRS) newsletter, this article is apparently based on a talk given to a gathering of religious men. Available at http://www.catholic-jhb.org.za/articles/baptism. htm#BAPTISM%20IN%20THE%20HOLY%20SPIRIT

7. Has there been a time in your life when you felt like the plug was pulled and the Spirit was allowed to flow in your life? How did that impact your Christian life?

In the following passage (Romans 8) St. Paul teaches on our relationship with the Holy Spirit and how it impacts our life. He often refers to "the flesh" in this passage. In the two previous chapters he explained that "the flesh" represents the weak, selfish side of human nature that is set against God. [6] Again, this should not be confused with the physical body.

Please invite a participant to read the following passage out loud:

Romans 8: 9-16, 26-27

[9] But you are not in the flesh, you are in the Spirit, if in fact the Spirit of God dwells in you. Any one who does not have the Spirit of Christ does not belong to him. [10] But if Christ is in you, although your bodies are dead because of sin, your spirits are alive because of righteousness. [11] If the Spirit of him who raised Jesus from the dead dwells in you, he who raised Christ Jesus from the dead will give life to your mortal bodies also through his Spirit which dwells in you. [12] So then, brethren, we are debtors, not to the flesh, to live according to the flesh -- [13] for if you live according to the flesh you will die, but if by the Spirit you put to death the deeds of the body you will live. [14] For all who are led by the Spirit of God are sons of God. [15] For you did not receive the spirit of slavery to fall back into fear, but you have received the spirit of sonship. When we cry, "Abba! Father!" [16] it is the Spirit himself bearing witness with our spirit that we are children of God...[26] Likewise the Spirit helps us in our weakness; for we do not know how to pray as we ought, but the Spirit himself intercedes for us with sighs too deep for words. [27] And he who searches the hearts of men knows what is the mind of the Spirit, because the Spirit intercedes for the saints according to the will of God.

---

[6]   Byrne, Brendan, S.J.; *Sacra Pagina: Romans* (ed. Daniel J. Harrington, S.J. ; The Liturgical Press: Collegeville, MN; 1996) p.227.

8. What names does Paul use for the Holy Spirit in this passage? How does this inform the way you think about the Holy Spirit?

9. Notice the word "in" every time Paul uses it in verses 9-11. What is the significance of this repetitiveness? What does it mean to you? Can you think of a word or phrase to substitute instead of "in"?

10. What are some of the effects of having the Spirit dwell in us?

11. What does it mean to "bear witness"? What do you think is the meaning of v.16? Have you ever experienced the Holy Spirit "bearing witness" with you? [7] Would you be willing to share that experience?

12. From this passage, what do you find most encouraging about the power of the Holy Spirit in your life? How can that impact your daily life?

The Catechism of the Catholic Church teaches that the Sacrament of Confirmation gives the Holy Spirit in a special way. If you have been confirmed, you may remember that when the Bishop signed your forehead with the sacred chrism, he said to you, "Be sealed with the Holy Spirit." The paragraph below explains the effects of the grace received in Confirmation.

1316 Confirmation perfects Baptismal grace; it is the sacrament which gives the Holy Spirit in order to root us more deeply in the divine filiation, incorporate us more firmly into Christ, strengthen our bond with

---

[7] Verse 16 is one of two places in Paul's writings where he uses the Aramaic "Abba" to describe our address to God in the Spirit. This is interesting because Paul's letters are written in Greek. Many scholars have discussed Paul's reason for not translating the word "Abba" into Greek. Some suggest that the word's resistance against translation suggests a word that was precious to the early Christian community. In Galations 4:6 Paul directly attributes this address of the Father to Jesus. We also see it placed on the lips of Jesus in Mark 14:36. Given this, scholars think that using the Aramaic "Abba" may have been a way for the early Christian community to enter into Jesus' intimate relationship with the Father—addressing God with the same exact word Jesus used while he was walking the earth. For more on this theory, see p. 250 and pp. 252-253 of Byrne's *Sacra Pagina: Romans*.

the Church, associate us more closely with her mission, and help us bear witness to the Christian faith in words accompanied by deeds.

13. What was your experience of Confirmation? Did you experience the reality of this grace at the time?

14. Have you experienced it at any time since your Confirmation?

Your Life and Mission

If you are baptized, you have been given the Holy Spirit. If you are confirmed, you have been sealed with the Holy Spirit and sent to the world to love it and serve it with the Spirit of Christ. The first step to living in this amazing reality is to acknowledge the Spirit's presence in you. You can do this by praying specifically to the Holy Spirit—perhaps a simple prayer of thanks and openness.

Here are some ways to grow closer to the Holy Spirit in your life:

- Pray the prayer to the Holy Spirit (found at the end of this session) everyday this week before you take your first bite to eat.

- Write the Bishop's prayer from the Rite of Confirmation in the text box from this session on an index card. Change the prayer to speak about you. For example, "you freed me from sin and gave me new life…" Hang it on your bathroom mirror and pray it every morning and evening.

- If there is a "Life in the Spirit" seminar or an event sponsored by local Catholics, you might consider attending it to experience the Holy Spirit in a new way.

- Try to find a Confirmation Mass to attend. Pay close attention to the rituals, promises, and commissioning. Pray for the individuals receiving the sacrament and also let the prayers renew your own Confirmation.

- Ask for the Holy Spirit to speak to you before reading Scripture and attending daily Mass this week.

In the Sacrament of Confirmation the Bishop extends his hands over the confirmandis and prays:

All-powerful God, Father of our Lord Jesus Christ, by water and the Holy Spirit you freed your sons and daughters from sin and gave them new life. Send your Holy Spirit upon them to be their helper and guide. Give them the spirit of wisdom and under-standing, the spirit of right judgment and courage, the spirit of knowledge and reverence. Fill them with the spirit of wonder and awe in your presence. We ask this through Christ our Lord.

You may also want to read more about the Holy Spirit in the Catechism of the Catholic Church. The primary teaching is found starting in paragraph 687, as the Church teaches on the Creed's statements on the Holy Spirit. You can find many more explanations by looking at the index of the *Catechism*.

Closing Prayer

Fr. Cantalamessa said that these sacraments are untied through faith. Use the opportunity of this prayer to tell the Lord you believe in his great love and wonderful promises. Invite the Holy Spirit to dwell within you in a new way as you pray this traditional prayer of the Church to the Holy Spirit.

Come Holy Spirit,
Fill the hearts of your faithful,
And enkindle in us the fire of your love.
Send forth Your Spirit and we shall be created,
And You shall renew the face of the earth.

O God, you instructed the hearts of the faithful.
By the light of the Holy Spirit,
Grant us in the same Spirit,
To be truly wise,
And ever to rejoice in His consolation.
Through Christ our Lord. Amen.

[Facilitator]: St. Paul

[Group members]: Pray for us.

CHURCH

WEEK 6

"We, though many, are one body in Christ, and individually members one of another."

Romans 12:5

Opening Prayer

Have someone read the following passage aloud, then pray the prayer altogether.

2 Timothy 1:6-8

[6]Hence I remind you to rekindle the gift of God that is within you through the laying on of my hands; [7]for God did not give us a spirit of timidity but a spirit of power and love and self-control. [8]Do not be ashamed then of testifying to our Lord, nor of me his prisoner, but share in suffering for the gospel in the power of God.

Almighty God, through our Confirmation, we, like your servant Timothy, experienced the apostolic laying on of hands that leads to service in your Church. We rejoice in the sacraments, that the hands of the bishops who confirmed us bear the gifts and power Christ imparted to the apostles. Enkindle the fire of your Holy Spirit we received in baptism and embraced at Confirmation. Help us to experience with new depth and intensity the power of your Holy Spirit for building up ourselves and our Church. Take away any timidity in our hearts. Give us through your Holy Spirit the power, the love and the self-control to become Christians who inspire others to love and serve your Son. We ask this through your Son, Christ Our Lord. Amen.

Paul's Life and Mission

Acts 27: 27 – 44, 28: 1 – 16

²⁷When the fourteenth night had come, as we were drifting across the sea of A'dria, about midnight the sailors suspected that they were nearing land. ²⁸So they sounded and found twenty fathoms; a little farther on they sounded again and found fifteen fathoms. ²⁹And fearing that we might run on the rocks, they let out four anchors from the stern, and prayed for day to come. ³⁰And as the sailors were seeking to escape from the ship, and had lowered the boat into the sea, under pretense of laying out anchors from the bow, ³¹Paul said to the centurion and the soldiers, "Unless these men stay in the ship, you cannot be saved." ³²Then the soldiers cut away the ropes of the boat, and let it go. ³³As day was about to dawn, Paul urged them all to take some food, saying, "Today is the fourteenth day that you have continued in suspense and without food, having taken nothing. ³⁴Therefore I urge you to take some food; it will give you strength, since not a hair is to perish from the head of any of you." ³⁵And when he had said this, he took bread, and giving thanks to God in the presence of all he broke it and began to eat. ³⁶Then they all were encouraged and ate some food themselves. ³⁷(We were in all two hundred and seventy-six persons in the ship.) ³⁸And when they had eaten enough, they lightened the ship, throwing out the wheat into the sea. ³⁹Now when it was day, they did not recognize the land, but they noticed a bay with a beach, on which they planned if possible to bring the ship ashore. ⁴⁰So they cast off the anchors and left them in the sea, at the same time loosening the ropes that tied the rudders; then hoisting the foresail to the wind they made for the beach. ⁴¹But striking a shoal they ran the vessel aground; the bow stuck and remained immovable, and the stern was broken up by the surf. ⁴²The soldiers' plan was to kill the prisoners, lest any should swim away and escape; ⁴³but the centurion, wishing to save Paul, kept them from carrying out their purpose. He ordered those who could

swim to throw themselves overboard first and make for the land, ⁴⁴and the rest on planks or on pieces of the ship. And so it was that all escaped to land.

¹After we had escaped, we then learned that the island was called Malta. ²And the natives showed us unusual kindness, for they kindled a fire and welcomed us all, because it had begun to rain and was cold. ³Paul had gathered a bundle of sticks and put them on the fire, when a viper came out because of the heat and fastened on his hand. ⁴When the natives saw the creature hanging from his hand, they said to one another, "No doubt this man is a murderer. Though he has escaped from the sea, justice has not allowed him to live." ⁵He, however, shook off the creature into the fire and suffered no harm. ⁶They waited, expecting him to swell up or suddenly fall down dead; but when they had waited a long time and saw no misfortune come to him, they changed their minds and said that he was a god. ⁷Now in the neighborhood of that place were lands belonging to the chief man of the island, named Publius, who received us and entertained us hospitably for three days. ⁸It happened that the father of Publius lay sick with fever and dysentery; and Paul visited him and prayed, and putting his hands on him healed him. ⁹And when this had taken place, the rest of the people on the island who had diseases also came and were cured. ¹⁰They presented many gifts to us; and when we sailed, they put on board whatever we needed.

1. Has fear ever made you want to "abandon ship?" What are the implications of escaping the ship?

2. Paul doesn't want anyone to leave the ship, because they will die. This can be seen as a model of Church. Catholics understand themselves as saved collectively, as the ecclesia, as the gathering of the faithful. God modeled this in the covenant with the Jewish people. The Church is the means to our salvation. This doesn't mean we neglect responding individually to God and striving to live as disciples, but that our salvation is intricately interwoven with one another. In what ways is Paul "church" to the others on board the ship?

3. What is the response of the sailors and others on board to sharing a meal? Do you ever feel anything similar?

4. Why do you think the centurion wanted to spare Paul's life? What experience of "church" would have prompted him to risk violating the usual military procedures?

5. Are the Maltese "church" to Paul and the sailors? In what way are they, and in what way do they fail to be? How is Paul church for them?

Have someone read the following passage aloud.

Romans 12:3 – 13

³For by the grace given to me I bid every one among you not to think of himself more highly than he ought to think, but to think with sober judgment, each according to the measure of faith which God has assigned him. ⁴For as in one body we have many members, and all the members do not have the same function, ⁵so we, though many, are one body in Christ, and individually members one of another. ⁶Having gifts that differ according to the grace given to us, let us use them: if prophecy, in proportion to our faith; ⁷if service, in our serving; he who teaches, in his teaching; ⁸he who exhorts, in his exhortation; he who contributes, in liberality; he who gives aid, with zeal; he who does acts of mercy, with cheerfulness. ⁹Let love be genuine; hate what is evil, hold fast to what is good; ¹⁰love one another with brotherly affection; outdo one another in showing honor. ¹¹Never flag in zeal, be aglow with the Spirit, serve the Lord. ¹²Rejoice in your hope, be patient in tribulation, be constant in prayer. ¹³ Contribute to the needs of the saints, practice hospitality.

6. Often, these sorts of teachings arise out of a community's conflict. What sort of conflict do you think St. Paul was addressing among the church in Rome?

7. Have you seen the gifts Paul lists manifested in your community? Can you describe individuals who seem to be living their gift particularly fruitfully?

8. How could you use St. Paul's image of the "body of Christ" as a way of explaining the structure of the Catholic Church? What part of the body are the Pope, Bishops, Priests, Deacons, Parishioners, Religious Orders, Cloistered Monks, Service Organizations, Evangelical and Catechetical Organizations, etc.? [8]

9. What gifts do you think God has given you for the good of the church and the world?

10. How would Paul's advice to "outdo one another in showing honor" help us in our jobs and our service at our local parish?

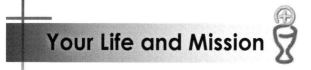

Your Life and Mission

This week try to be church to others in the ways we saw Paul, the sailors and the Maltese being church. What concrete actions can you take to make this happen? Plan ahead.

Look at 1 Corinthians 12 and the reading from Lumen Gentium in the appendix in order to meditate more deeply on how we can build up the Church through our lives.

Take time to pray for someone who is thinking about abandoning the ship of the Catholic Church. Pray that they would recognize and embrace the promises given to those that remain onboard. Pray also that they would find peace with the situations or people that are driving them off the ship.

Using what you know from this study of St. Paul's life and struggles as a leader of the Church, pray specifically for your local bishop and pastor. Pray that they would be filled with the love of God, that they would resist temptation, live lives of virtue, endure suffering, be filled with the Spirit, and faithful to the task of building up the body of Christ.

---

[8]   The Appendix contains a pertinent reading from the Second Vatican Council's Dogmatic Constitution on the Church (Lumen Gentium).

Closing Prayer

Read the following passage aloud together. We began this series by reading Pope Benedict's encouragement to think of what St. Paul was speaking to us today. We trust that he has been praying for us every week as we gathered. Now, let us hear in this closing passage of Scripture, the caring words of St. Paul to us individually. He continues to be our teacher, Apostle, and herald.

Philippians 1:3-11

³I thank my God in all my remembrance of you, ⁴always in every prayer of mine for you all making my prayer with joy, ⁵thankful for your partnership in the gospel from the first day until now. ⁶And I am sure that he who began a good work in you will bring it to completion at the day of Jesus Christ. ⁷It is right for me to feel thus about you all, because I hold you in my heart, for you are all partakers with me of grace, both in my imprisonment and in the defense and confirmation of the gospel. ⁸For God is my witness, how I yearn for you all with the affection of Christ Jesus. ⁹And it is my prayer that your love may abound more and more, with knowledge and all discernment, ¹⁰so that you may approve what is excellent, and may be pure and blameless for the day of Christ, ¹¹filled with the fruits of righteousness which come through Jesus Christ, to the glory and praise of God.

We thank you Lord for the witness and teaching of your faithful servant St. Paul. May our lives reflect the faith we have studied during these six weeks. May our Church be faithful to the foundation that was laid so carefully by St. Paul and the other apostles. We pray this through Jesus Christ, our Lord. Amen.

[Facilitator]: St. Paul

[Group members]: Pray for us.

Small Group Discussion Guidelines

A small Christian community seeks to foster a deeper and more meaningful connection with God and with one another. For many of you this will no doubt be a new experience. You may be wondering what will take place, will I fit in, and even will I want to come back? These are fair considerations. Here are some expectations and values to help clarify what this community will be about. Please read the following aloud and discuss if necessary:

Purpose

We gather as Christians – our express purpose in gathering is to encourage one another in our mutual commitment to living the Gospel of Jesus Christ in and through the Church.

Priority

In order to reap the full fruits of this personal and communal journey of faith, we will make participation in the weekly gatherings a priority.

Participation

Each person has a unique relationship with God. We will strive to create an environment in which all are encouraged to share at their comfort level.

Discussion Guidelines

The heart of our gathering time is our sharing in "Spirit-filled" discussion. This type of dialogue occurs when the presence of the Holy Spirit is welcomed and encouraged by the nature and tenor of the discussion. To engage in such a discussion, we will observe the following guidelines:

- Participants give constant attention to respect, humility, openness, and honesty in sharing.

- Participants share on their level of personal comfort.

- As silence is a vital part of the total process, participants are given time to reflect before sharing begins. Also, keep in mind that a period of comfortable silence often occurs between individual sharing.

- Participants are enthusiastically encouraged to share while, at the same time, exercising care to permit others (especially the quieter members) an opportunity to share. Each participant should aim to maintain a balance between participating joyfully and not dominating the conversation.

- Participants are to respect with confidentiality anything of a personal nature that may have been shared in the group.

- Perhaps most importantly, participants should seek to cultivate a mindfulness of the Holy Spirit's desire to be present in the time spent together.

Time

It is important that your group starts and ends on time. Generally a group meets for about 90 minutes with an additional 30 minutes or so for refreshments. Agree on these times as a group and work to honor them.

Your Role
as a Facilitator

Perhaps no skill is more important to the success of your small group than the ability to facilitate a discussion according to the movement of the Holy Spirit. Such an approach recognizes the prominence of God's sanctifying Spirit in the spiritual journey, not necessarily our knowledge or theological acumen. The following guidelines can help facilitators avoid some of the common pitfalls of small group discussion, and open the door for the Spirit to take the lead in the "connection" we seek with Jesus Christ.

You are a Facilitator, NOT a Teacher

It can be incredibly tempting to answer every question as a facilitator. You may have excellent answers and be excited about sharing them with your brothers and sisters in Christ. However, a more Socratic method, by which you attempt to draw answers from participants, is much more fruitful in the long run. Get in the habit of reflecting participants' questions to the whole group before offering your own input. It is not necessary for you as a facilitator to immediately enter into the discussion or offer a magisterial answer. Matter of fact, when others have sufficiently addressed an issue, try to exercise restraint in your comments. Simply affirm what has been said, thank them, and move on. If you don't know the answer to a given question, have a participant look it up in the Catechism of the Catholic Church and have them read it aloud to the group. If you cannot find an answer, ask someone to research the question and bring their discoveries to the next session. Finally, never feel embarrassed to say, "I don't know." Simply acknowledge the quality of the question and offer to follow up with that person after some digging. Remember, you are a facilitator, not a teacher.

Affirm and Encourage

We are more likely to repeat a behavior when it is openly encouraged. If you want to encourage more active participation and sharing, give positive affirmation to group members' responses. This is especially important if people are sharing from their heart. A simple "thank you for sharing that" can go a long way in encouraging further discussion in your small group. If someone has offered a theologically question-able response, don't be nervous or combative. Wait until others have offered their input. It is very likely that someone will offer a more helpful response, after which you can affirm them by saying something like, "That is the typical Christian perspective on that topic. Thank you." If no acceptable response is given, and you know the answer, exercise great care and respect in your comments so as not to ap-pear smug or self-righteous. You might begin with something like, "Those are all interesting perspectives. What the Church has said about this is. . ."

Avoid Unhelpful Tangents

There is nothing that can derail a Spirit-filled discussion more quickly than digressing into unnecessary tangents. Try to keep the session on track. If the group gets off on a tangent, ask yourself, "Is this a Spirit-guided tangent?" If not, bring the group back by asking a question that steers conversation back to center. You may even have to suggest kind-ly, "Have we gotten a little off topic?" Most participants will respond positively and redirect according to your sensitive leading. That being said, some tangents may be worth pursuing if you sense the action of the Spirit. It may be exactly where God wants to steer the discussion. You'll find that taking risks can yield some beautiful results.

Fear NOT the Silence

Be okay with silence. Most people need a moment or two to muster up a response to a question. It is quite natural to need some time to formulate our thoughts and put them into words. Some may need a moment just to conjure up the courage to speak at all. Regardless of the reason, do not be afraid of a brief moment of silence after asking a question. Let everyone in the group know early on that silence is an integral part of normal discussion, and that they shouldn't worry or be uncomfortable when it happens. This applies to times of prayer as well. If no one shares or prays after a sufficient amount of time, just move on gracefully.

The Power of Hospitality

It is amazing how far a little hospitality can go. Everybody likes to be cared for and this is especially true in a small group whose purpose it is to connect to Jesus Christ, our model for care, support, and compassion. Make a point to greet people personally when they first arrive. Ask them how their day was. Take some time to invest in the lives of your small group participants. Work at remembering each person's name. Help everyone feel comfortable and at home. Allow your small group to be an environment where authentic relationships take shape and blossom.

Encourage Participation

Help everyone to get involved, especially those who are naturally less vocal or outgoing. A good way to encourage participation initially is to always invite participants to read the selected readings aloud. Down the road, even after the majority of the group feels comfortable sharing, you'll still have some quieter members who may not always volunteer a response to a question but would be happy to read.

Meteorology?

Keep an eye on what we call the "Holy Spirit barometer." Is the discussion pleasing to the Holy Spirit? Is this conversation leading participants to a deeper personal connection to Jesus Christ? The intellectual aspects of our faith are certainly important to discuss, but conversation can sometimes degenerate into an unedifying showcase of intellect and ego. Discussion can sometimes take a negative turn and become a venue for gossip, complaining, or even slander. You can almost feel the Holy Spirit leave the room when this happens! If you are aware that this dynamic has taken over a particular discussion, take a moment to pray quietly in your heart, asking the Holy Spirit to help you bring it back around. This can often be achieved simply by moving on to the next question.

Pace

Generally, you want to pace the study to finish in the allotted time, but sometimes this may be impossible without sacrificing quality discussion. If you reach the end of your meeting and find you have only covered half the material, don't fret! This is often the result of lively Spirit-filled discussion and meaningful theological reflection. In this case you may want to take another meeting to cover the remainder of the material. If you only have a small portion left, you can ask participants to finish it on their own and to come to the following meeting with any questions or insights they have. Even if you have to skip a section to end on time, make sure you leave adequate time for prayer and to review the "Connecting to Christ This Week" section. This is vital in helping participants integrate their discoveries from the group into their daily lives.

Joy

Remember that seeking the face of the Lord is a joyful process! There is nothing more fulfilling, more illuminating, and more beautiful than to foster a deep and enduring relationship with Jesus Christ. Embrace your participants and the entire spiritual journey with a spirit of joyful anticipation of what God wants to accomplish through your small group.

> These things I have spoken to you,
> that my joy may be in you,
> and that your joy may be full.
> John 15:11

Materials to Have
at your Small Group

Several materials may be very helpful to have on hand while facilitating your small group:

Bible

You and all members of the small group should bring a Bible to each session. It's a good idea to bring extras, if you can, for those who might forget. We recommend the New American Bible, the Catholic Study Bible, the New Jerusalem Bible, which has excellent footnotes, or The Catholic Serendipity Bible, which is not as scholarly, but contains good devotional material.

Catechism of the Catholic Church

Most sessions include reading selections from the Catechism, all of which are printed out in text for your convenience. However, you will want to have at least one Catechism at hand for referencing when questions come up in discussion. You might encourage all of your participants to purchase one for their own collection, as it is an invaluable resource for private study and reflection.

A Theological Dictionary

We recommend Image Book's The Pocket Catholic Dictionary by John A. Hardon, S.J. It offers concise definitions for a panoply of Catholic terms. As you are preparing for your small group, you may decide to make other materials available for purchase, such as some of the classic writings of the Catholic tradition listed in the Appendix. We have found this to be a great way to get good books into the hands of eager people.

APPENDIX A

A Guide to the
Sacrament of Reconciliation

If it has been a long time since you last "went to confession," you may be hesitant and unsure. Join the club! However, reconciling with God is always a cause of great joy in our lives. Take the plunge! You'll be glad you did. Below is a step-by-step description of the process that may help alleviate your fears. Keep in mind that you always have the option to go to confession privately behind a screen or face-to-face with the priest.

1. Prepare to receive the sacrament by praying and examining your conscience, perhaps with a tool such as the ones included in the appendices of this booklet.
2. Begin by making the Sign of the Cross and greeting the priest by saying, "Bless me father, for I have sinned," and telling the priest how long it has been since your last confession.
3. Confess your sins to the priest. If you are unsure about something, ask him to help you. Place your trust in God, a merciful and loving father. When you are finished, indicate this by saying something like, "I am sorry for these and all of my sins."
4. The priest will assign you a penance such as prayer or a work of mercy, service or sacrifice.
5. Express sorrow for your sins by saying an act of contrition such as the one below.
6. The priest, acting in the person of Christ, will absolve you from your sins by saying the Prayer of Absolution, to which you respond by making the Sign of the Cross and saying, "Amen."
7. The priest will offer some proclamation of praise, such as "Give thanks to the Lord, for he is good," to which you respond, "His mercy endures forever."
8. The priest will dismiss you.
9. Go and complete your assigned penance.

An Act of Contrition

O my God, I am heartily sorry for having offended you and I detest all my sins, not only because I dread the loss of heaven and pains of hell, but most of all because they offend you, my God, who are all good and deserving of all my love. I firmly resolve, with the help of your grace, to confess my sins, to do penance, and to amend my life.
Amen.

APPENDIX B

An Examination of Conscience

Based on the words of Jesus and St. Paul

The examination may be read silently as you prepare for your confession.

> Jesus said: "You shall love the Lord, your God,With all your heart, with all your soul, and with all your mind.This is the greatest commandment.The second is like it:You shall love your neighbor as yourself." -Mt 22:37-40

Love is patient, love is kind. . .

* Do I love the Lord with all my heart, soul and mind, or do I hold back because of my love of possessions or status or because of my own fear?
* Do I express my love for God with daily prayer and participation in the Mass? Do I express my patience and trust in the Lord by keeping Sunday as a holy day?
* Do I patiently wait for the Lord to hear my prayers, or do I take things into my own hands? Have I truly given the reigns of my life to God or am I trying to maintain control?
* Am I putting into practice those things God is calling me to do?
* Am I patient with my family, friends and co-workers?
* Do I treat others with true kindness? Am I generous with my time? Do I share my gifts with those in need?
* Am I true to my family relationships? To my friends? Do I act or speak one way in their presence and another when they are gone?
* Do I honor my parents and show them respect and love?
* Do I empathize with others, especially those who are poor and vulnerable or who seem difficult to love?
* Do I dishonor my body by fornication, impurity, unworthy conversation, lustful thoughts, evil desires or actions? Have I given in to sensuality? Have I indulged in reading, conversation, shows, and entertainment that offends Christian decency?

> "[The sacrament of Reconciliation] is called the sacrament of conversion because it makes sacramentally present Jesus' call to conversion, the first step in returning to the Father from whom one has strayed by sin." -CCC, 1423

Love is not jealous, it is not pompous, it is not inflated, it is not rude. . .

- Am I jealous of other people? Do I covet their popularity, wealth, possessions or abilities?
- Do I look down on others of different financial status or social class?
- Am I quick to judge others?
- Do I treat all people with respect and love?
- Do I interrupt people in conversation? Do my own thoughts, ideas and words take precedence over others'?
- Love does not seek its own interests, it is not quick-tempered, it does not brood over injury. . .
- Do I put aside my own wishes and desires to serve God, as well as my family, parish, and community?
- Do I become angry if things don't go "my way?"
- Am I quick to speak harshly to others? To strangers? To those I love?
- Am I able to truly forgive others? Or do I hang onto pain and mistrust?
- Do I brood over wrongs others commit?
- Have I committed violence against others? Have I struck someone in anger? Am I abusive – physically or emotionally – of a spouse or child? Have I been involved with abortion?
- Have I stolen from someone or kept something that does not belong to me?
- Have I been faithful to my spouse?
- Have I had recourse to artificial contraception or sterilization?

Love does not rejoice over wrongdoing but rejoices with the truth. . .

- Do I rejoice in other's achievements or am I left threatened or defensive? Do I often highlight the negative in others' lives to make me feel better? Am I somehow pleased when others fail or are wronged?
- Do I expect the best of the worst from other people?
- Do I cherish the truth above all things or only when it is convenient or advantageous for me? Am I true to my own word?
- Do I gossip? Lie? Cheat?

> "Whoever confesses his sins . . . is already working with God. God indicts your sins; if you also indict them, you are joined with God." -St. Augustine.

Love bears all things, believes all things, hopes all things, endures all things. . .

- Do I endure hardships in my life with patience, hope and joy in the Lord?
- Do I believe the tenants of the Catholic faith?
- Does my love of Christ compel me to live out the Church's beliefs in all facets of my life?
- Do I wait in joyful hope for our Lord's return in glory?
- Am I hopeful, even in the midst of the world's uncertainty?
- Do I try to manage the trials of my life on my own or by faith in God's goodness and provision? Am I willing to bear my own crosses as I follow in the footsteps of Jesus?

A Prayer of the Penitent

Lord Jesus, you chose to be called the friend of sinners.
By your saving death and resurrection free me from my sins.
May your peace take root in my heart and bring forth a harvest
Of love, holiness, and truth. Amen.
- *from the Rite of Penance*

APPENDIX C

God's Love in the
Catechism of the Catholic Church

God's Love in the Catechism of the Catholic Church

218 In the course of its history, Israel was able to discover that God had only one reason to reveal himself to them, a single motive for choosing them from among all peoples as his special possession: his sheer gratuitous love. And thanks to the prophets Israel understood that it was again out of love that God never stopped saving them and pardoning their unfaithfulness and sins.

219 God's love for Israel is compared to a father's love for his son. His love for his people is stronger than a mother's for her children. God loves his people more than a bridegroom his beloved; his love will be victorious over even the worst infidelities and will extend to his most precious gift: "God so loved the world that he gave his only Son."

220 God's love is "everlasting": "For the mountains may depart and the hills be removed, but my steadfast love shall not depart from you." Through Jeremiah, God declares to his people, "I have loved you with an everlasting love; therefore I have continued my faithfulness to you."[43]

221 But St. John goes even further when he affirms that "God is love": God's very being is love. By sending his only Son and the Spirit of Love in the fullness of time, God has revealed his innermost secret: God himself is an eternal exchange of love, Father, Son and Holy Spirit, and he has destined us to share in that exchange.

> • **What parallels do you see between the passages we looked at in the session on Love and the passages the Catechism uses in the above paragraphs?**

APPENDIX D

Dogmatic Constitution
on the Church *(Lumen Gentium)*

Teaching relating to the Body of Christ

---

7. In the human nature united to Himself the Son of God, by over-coming death through His own death and resurrection, redeemed man and re-molded him into a new creation.(50) By communicating His Spirit, Christ made His brothers, called together from all nations, mys-tically the components of His own Body.

As all the members of the human body, though they are many, form one body, so also are the faithful in Christ.(56) Also, in the building up of Christ's Body various members and functions have their part to play. There is only one Spirit who, according to His own richness and the needs of the ministries, gives His different gifts for the welfare of the Church.(57) What has a special place among these gifts is the grace of the apostles to whose authority the Spirit Himself subjected even those who were endowed with charisms.(58) Giving the body unity through Himself and through His power and inner joining of the members, this same Spirit produces and urges love among the be-lievers. From all this it follows that if one member endures anything, all the members co-endure it, and if one member is honored, all the members together rejoice.(59)

The Head of this Body is Christ. He is the image of the invisible God and in Him all things came into being. He is before all creatures and in Him all things hold together. He is the head of the Body which is the Church. He is the beginning, the firstborn from the dead, that in all things He might have the first place.(60) By the greatness of His power He rules the things in heaven and the things on earth, and with His all-surpassing perfection and way of acting He fills the whole body with the riches of His glory.

From Him "the whole body, supplied and built up by joints and liga-ments, attains a growth that is of God".(65) He continually distributes in His body, that is, in the Church, gifts of ministries in which, by His own power, we serve each other unto salvation so that, carrying out the truth in love, we might through all things grow unto Him who is our Head.(66)

In order that we might be unceasingly renewed in Him,(67) He has shared with us His Spirit who, existing as one and the same being in the Head and in the members, gives life to, unifies and moves through the whole body. This He does in such a way that His work could be compared by the holy Fathers with the function which the principle of life, that is, the soul, fulfills in the human body.(8*)

APPENDIX D

Gift of Tongues

The following paragraph from the Catechism shows that the Church today acknowledges the existence of a special gift of tongues given by the Holy Spirit.

2003 Grace is first and foremost the gift of the Spirit who justifies and sanctifies us. But grace also includes the gifts that the Spirit grants us to associate us with his work, to enable us to collaborate in the salvation of others and in the growth of the Body of Christ, the Church. There are sacramental graces, gifts proper to the different sacraments. There are furthermore special graces, also called charisms after the Greek term used by St. Paul and meaning "favor," "gratuitous gift," "benefit." Whatever their character - sometimes it is extraordinary, such as the gift of miracles or of tongues - charisms are oriented toward sanctifying grace and are intended for the common good of the Church. They are at the service of charity which builds up the Church.

The following is on the gift of tongues from other various sources.

The gift of tongues and (5) the interpretation of tongues (collectively known as glossolalia) are described at length in 1 Corinthians 14. In what did glossolalia exactly consist?

• It was speaking, opposed to being silent (1 Corinthians 14:28), yet not always in a foreign tongue. On the day of Pentecost the Apostles did indeed speak the various languages of their hearers, but the still unbaptized Gentiles in the house of Cornelius "speaking with tongues, and magnifying God" (Acts 10:46) and the twelve newly baptized Ephesians speaking with tongues and prophesying (Acts 19:6) had no reason for using any strange tongue. Again, instead of the expression "speaking with tongues" Paul uses the alternative phrases, "speaking in a tongue", "by a tongue", "with a tongue" (1 Corinthians 14:2, 4, 13, 14, 27). The object of the gift was not to convey ideas to listeners, but to speak to God in prayer (ibid., 2, 4), an object for which a foreign language is unnecessary. Lastly -- and this argument seems conclusive

-- Paul compares glossolalia, as regards its effect, with talking in an unknown language; it is, therefore, not itself an unknown language (ibid., 11).

- It was an articulate language, for the speaker prays, sings, gives thanks (ibid., 14-17).

- The speaker was in a kind of trance -- "If I pray in a tongue, my spirit [pneuma] prayeth, but my understanding [nous, mens] is without fruit" (ibid., 14).

- On unbelievers glossolalia made the impression of the marvellous; perhaps it recalled to their mind the religious ravings of hierophants: "Wherefore (i.e. because unintelligible) tongues are for a sign, not to believers, but to unbelievers. If . . . all speak with tongues, and there come in unlearned persons or infidels, will they not say that you are mad?" (1 Corinthians 14:22, 23).

- The gift of tongues is inferior to that of prophecy: "Greater is he that prophesieth, than he that speaketh with tongues: unless perhaps he interpret, that the church may receive edification" (ibid., 5).

- The charisma of interpretation is, then, the necessary complement of glossolalia; when interpretation is not forthcoming, the speaker with tongues shall hold his peace (ibid., 13, 27, 28). Interpretation-form of an intelligible address; the explanation was to follow the speech with tongues as regularly as the discerning of spirits succeeded prophecy (1 Corinthians 14:28, 29). is the work either of the speaker himself or of another (ibid., 27).

Among the Fathers it is sententia communissima that the speaking with tongues was a speaking in foreign languages. Their interpretation is based upon the promise in Mark 16:1, "They shall speak with new tongues", and on its final fulfilment in the gift of tongues to the apostles (Acts 2:4). A new tongue, however, is not necessarily a foreign language, and a gift which had a special use on the day of Pentecost appears purposeless in meetings of people of one language. There are, besides, textual objections to the common opinion, although, it must be owned, not quite convincing [see the second point above]. Many explanations of this obscure charisma are proposed, but not one of them is free from objection. It may indeed be that there is some truth in all of them. St. Paul speaks of "kinds of tongues", which may imply that glossolalia manifested itself in many forms: e.g. in the form of foreign languages when required by circumstances, as with the Apostles; as a new language -- "a kind of speech distinctive of the spiritual life and distinguished from common speech, which to the exuberant feeling of the new faith appeared unsuitable for intercourse with God" (Weizsacker); or as the manifestation of the unspeakable groanings of the Spirit, asking for us, and causing us to cry, "Abba, Father" (Romans 8:15, 26).

I Cor., xii-xiv, with commentaries; ST. THOMAS, II-II, QQ. clxxvi-clxxviii; ENGLMANN, Die Charismen (Ratisbon, 1848 -- best book on the subject); SCHRAM, Theol. mystica, 435; SEISENBERGER in Kirchenlex., s. v.; ID. In BUCHBERGER, Kirchl. Handlexikon; WEIZSACKER, Apost. Age, II, 254-75.

Wilhelm, Joseph. "Charismata." The Catholic Encyclopedia. Vol. 3. New York: Robert Appleton Company, 1908. 12 Sept. 2008 <http://www.newadvent.org/cathen/03588e.htm>.

Ecclesiastical approbation. Nihil Obstat. November 1, 1908. Remy Lafort, S.T.D., Censor. Imprimatur. +John Cardinal Farley, Archbishop of New York.

the
evangelical
catholic
forming disciples.
training leaders.

Made in the
USA
Columbia, SC